SETTING THEM FREE: NOTES ON TEACHING

ROGER SIMPSON

ISBN: 978-0-9963736-2-3
Copyright 2015 by Roger Simpson

All rights reserved. Except for use in any review, the reproduction or utilization of this work in whole or in part in any form by any electronic, mechanical or other means, now known or hereafter invented, including xerography, photocopying and recording, or in any information storage or retrieval system, is forbidden without the written permission of the publisher, Summerland Publishing, 887 Hanson Street, Bozeman, MT 59718.

This book is based on the author's experiences as a university instructor. The names, places, dates, sequences, or the detail of events have been altered to protect the privacy of others.

Printed in the United States of America.

Library of Congress #2015954941

"Flight of the Wild Geese" cover art and *"Little Girl in the Sky"* art and story by Leonardo Katz

Skill is almost always fatal to feeling.
Eugene Delacroix

The Little Girl in the Sky

We were all sitting over little desks drawing in crayon. It was somewhere back in the second or third grade. The teacher was walking around the room looking at each kid's drawing and commenting on it.

When she got to the girl behind me I heard her say, "You've got that little girl standing in the sky! You have to continue the grass behind her – see, like this." I immediately picked up my green crayon to fill in the grass behind my little boy who, just a moment before, was also standing in the sky.

I dodged the bullet, as they say, but the price I paid in that moment of instruction was the loss of a child's pure and innocent creativity.

I can't stand to sing the same song the same way two nights in succession. If you can, it ain't music, it's close order drill, or exercise or yodeling or something, not music.
Billie Holiday

A few years back, there was this talent contest for kids on local television. The usual corny and cute singing and dancing performances. I don't remember any of the contestants except for one little girl. She was a local girl, about ten or eleven, and she belted out her numbers with such verve and fearlessness, and then when everyone cheered she broke into the most open, joyful smile…it was a smile that no grown-up could, or if they could, would dare! It was too revealing, too innocent, too uncool. It was a sheer explosion of joy. It tore my heart out! I made a note to remember that little girl. She seemed born to perform.

A couple of years ago, I happened to tune in to a Honolulu station. There was a local girl singing with a band. It was her. All grown. She was a young lady now. It was her, but it wasn't. She had the presence of a professional entertainer. She was dressed like one, she moved around holding the mic with poise…when she came to the part in the song with the "you," she pointed semi-seductively to the audience; when she sang the word "heart," she touched her breast; her smile was on cue, nothing revealing…she was now a professional entertainer.

Because of her great potential she had been sent to the Big Apple of the Pacific for professional training. She had been untaught spontaneity, innocence, childlike exuberance. In exchange was technique.

The young girl, who had once stood in the sky in childish exuberance, was now standing respectfully on the grass she had been instructed to paint behind her.

Table of Contents

Prologue..5
The First Day 7
Surfing and Shaping 12
Just Beautiful 14
Summer School Recovery? 16
Forming a Circle in the Grass After the Attack 21
The Chairman's Evaluation 24
The Recommended Example 27
The Race Card and Vietnam 28
The Petition... 33
The Exit Interview 36
My Supporters?.. 38
Joe Wood's Class: The Kid in the Hoody 40
Playing Jazz Trumpet and Reading Philosophy 43
Audi... 48
Sophie and the Preacher 52
Ronald Reagan: The Greatest Socialist President in History 56
Trashing Lilly.. 58
The Silencers... 60
Your Money or Your Education...62
Breathing, Eating a Cookie and Finding Rain in a Sheet of Paper 64
A Six Year Old's Wisdom.. 67
The Crippled Boy 69
Sitting With a World War II Veteran.. 71
I Think I'm a Liberal; Should I Buy a Gun? 73
I Was Wondering About My Grade 75
What Are Grades Anyway?.. 77
Afterward 79
From the Love of My Students 80

Imagination is more important than knowledge.

Albert Einstein

Dedicated to my wife and daughter, my students, and in memory of my mentor, a true man of integrity, Howard Zinn

And so all the answers that you seek are cellular recorded in your being! You want to know something? Ask Yourself! You want to know how to rise to the heights of your consciousness? Ask Yourself!
Bartholomew

Prologue

I have been fortunate in my life because I have worked at two jobs I loved and only two that I didn't. The former were working on the San Francisco cable car as a gripman (driver) and teaching. The latter were working for two corporations. Let's forget the last two and focus on the first two.

For me, being a gripman and a teacher were and still are the experience of romance, freedom and caring. The romance of the cable car was floating down the big Hyde Street hill at 5:30 in the morning with a light breeze blowing and the steel spans of the Golden Gate Bridge accentuated in fresh morning sun with a whole day of new life and adventure, and sometimes, caring. The romance of teaching is always a whole day of new life and adventure minus the Golden Gate Bridge. The freedom in both is not having to answer to any personalities who so often, and especially in the corporate world, live from lack rather than abundance. The caring is in passenger safety and the success of the students.

You pull back on the grip and suddenly you are chugging along at nine miles per hour with no one telling you how to drive the cable car. You close the door of your classroom and you are suddenly free of administrators and other educational bureaucrats in general. In that hour or hour and a half, you and your students are free to be yourselves. You can either free the students from government programs like Teaching to the Test and laws like No Child Left Behind or you can bind them to them and they will never be set free. The caring is in sensing the needs of both passengers and students and trying to support them as best you can and sometimes failing.

When I first began teaching, I didn't know how to free them. It took a lot of teaching by brave students to show me how.

By the grace of God, I exited the corporate world as one of the "downsized," which was the gift I needed to begin my romance, adventure and caring with education again. Twenty years before, I began to learn how to teach at San Francisco State University and through a very brief spell as a reader and teaching assistant at San Quentin prison.

I have lived most of my life in a beautiful coastal town with a community college overlooking the sea. It was there that I first applied and within a couple months received a call for an interview which would be the rebirth of my teaching career. It was only a short drive or walk to school and the first part of this book documents those times, mostly happy for the first couple of years.

As you will see from these vignettes, after a period of about three years, I was "discontinued" and found myself commuting 160 miles round trip to a new community college in a more rural, farm-based area further up the California coast and slightly inland, with a dominantly Hispanic student population and one of the highest per capita teen pregnancy rates in the United States. After twelve years, I continue to teach there, working for a man of insight who guides our department. The later vignettes are from this period. This is what I have experienced in the process of assisting in setting my students free.

I believe we live in a time where, as Albert Einstein once said, "The only thing that interferes with my learning is my education." My hope is that these vignettes will bring education and learning together by example. I hope too that I can follow Einstein's lead and advice: "If you can't explain it **simply**, you don't understand it well enough."

The First Day

From the days of least experience in teaching onward, I have always felt that the first day of a class, and all classes, should be the "giving" of a teacher to the class. It should be a time of truth telling that lets the students know who the teacher is and what he or she expects. Most important it is the beginning of building a trust between a teacher and his or her students and the students between each other. Without it there is only historical lockstep motivation that seldom creates trust, knowledge or anything but false motivation and a race for grades in a cut-throat competitive and non-learning environment. Building trust is not guaranteed to be a magic bullet, and some students it will never touch, but the effort must be made.

I am always the first one in class and acknowledge each student individually as they enter, even though I don't yet know their names: a practice that usually takes about five weeks.

When they are all seated, I begin not with the roll but with a question that leads us into our first encounter which sometimes, if I'm lucky, leads to a two-way conversation.

"Why am I here?" I gaze around the room waiting for an answer. Silence. "The answer isn't that I love teaching, need the money, have nothing else to do, want to impart knowledge (whatever that means) to you. It's none of those answers, though those are all good answers. So…" I pause. "Anybody got an idea why I am here? The answer is so close you can touch it!" Sometimes there is no response but sometimes I get lucky and get the answer I am looking for: "You're here because of us."

"Thank you, thank you! That's it! See how close that is? It's the person sitting next to you and yourself as well. I am here to serve you. That's my only job. Without you there would be no buildings or administrators or college, and I know that some people here may not treat you as if their job depended upon you, but it does. I'm here to try to help you succeed and that doesn't mean memorizing the facts and dates of U.S. history, but it does mean thinking of the consequences of those facts and dates. Have we learned from previous experiences in history or are just doing the same thing over again without having learned? Is history repeating itself? I want you to think about history, not memorize it, and its connections: past to present, present to future.

"I remember when I sat where you are. I remember how I got pretty beaten up by the educational system and its teachers. I have asked the same two questions to hundreds of students. I'd like to ask you folks the same questions, if it's okay with you." There are several nods.

"Okay, first, how many teachers within your experience of thirteen, fourteen, fifteen years of school could you really talk to? By that I mean how many could you talk to as a person, telling them what you really felt, not just having to still pretend that they were the teacher and you were the student? I'm not talking about make-believe, but being real. Can I have a show of hands?" The number never surprises me because it is always the same three or four out of a class of thirty to fifty students. "Thank you. Now the second question, how many could you trust?" The answer never changes; it was almost always zero.

"Amazing, huh? The answers never change. Doesn't paint a very bright picture of our education system, does it? So, our job is to change that here, but I want you to remember from the beginning, don't believe anything I say from now on unless you see me do it. If I say one thing and do another, I am a hypocrite and can't be trusted." Some of the kids look a little cockeyed at me as if they aren't sure what they just heard. "In fact, in twenty-six years in a classroom as a student, I can remember only one teacher I could sort of talk to as a semi-human being, so don't feel like the Lone Ranger; I remember what it was like. Here, you can speak your mind, say what you want to and though it may not be my opinion, I won't put a skull and crossbones next to your name on the roll sheet." They laugh. "I once had a teacher whom I tried to ask for a rereading of an exam that I thought was better than his grade. I had done the unthinkable and questioned his judgment. From then on he gave me straight F's to the midterm and straight A's to the final, so I got a C in the class. I have no agenda and that won't happen here. We must learn to respect each other's opinions, whatever they are, because each of you may have a contribution that none of us have ever heard before. Believe me, there are no answers or questions that are stupid when asked with sincerity. Remember that.

"Any questions?" So far there are none. "All right. I will do whatever I can to aid your success, but you have to share half of the responsibility. What does that mean? I will give you plenty of time to do assignments, so it's your responsibility to get them in on time. It is also in fairness to the majority of students that you do so. You have a responsibility to them: no excuses. Also, please, please don't shoot yourself in the foot by not turning in assignments because that will have a direct effect on your grade.

"Lectures are boring, no matter how good they are, so I will give a different person every class period a Hindu temple bell. Your job when you have the bell is to ring it every twenty minutes, and I will stop talking and we will take a stretch break and relax a minute or two, then continue. Many students feel uncomfortable doing this, but I'm the one asking you to do so. You may also feel uncomfortable calling me by my name, Roger. However, if that's too hard, just call me what makes you most comfortable.

Finally, if you have something to say, you don't have to raise your hand, just speak out; my experience is that unless it is in the midst of a heated discussion, students normally respect each other and wait until someone else finishes speaking. Some take to this right away and others don't all semester; do what is best for you.

"Also, don't hesitate to stop me if you haven't understood something or I am talking too fast. Let me know because the chances are that at least 60% of the class didn't understand either, usually because my explanation wasn't clear."

A student raised his hand. "Roger?" Some students appear startled that someone was already using my first name.

"Yes?"

"I'm looking at the assignment sheet and the syllabus and can't find a midterm, final or a textbook, just the four other books you've assigned. Am I missing something?"

I smile. "No, you've got it right. I find textbooks to be pretty confusing because they skip around: one chapter will end in 1877 and the next will begin in 1800; it's very confusing. So next time I will give you an historical chronology that will list all the important dates and a brief summary of most of the events. If you get lost, just look for a date. They are in order from the beginning to the current presidency. Also, I can give you three or four cutting edge, interesting books for a little more than half the cost of a textbook. These are books I value and hope you will too. Last, I never give midterms or finals because it goes-in-one-ear-and-out-the-other. I find that papers and quizzes are more effective and fulfilling. Any questions? Again, don't trust me unless I follow through on what I say."

As the students file out, I watch them talking to each other, some wondering if I am for real. Others wave good-bye, "See you next time,

Roger," trying out my first name for the first time. By midyear, 80% of my students will comfortably use my first name. It happens that way every year.

Surfing and Shaping

Jimmy, a student in one of the classes I first taught at the local community college, had just about finished his AA degree. It was near the end of his last semester when he dropped by the office. He was bright; his mind could ferret out the details in an overview of the whole picture.

"So, what can I do for you?"

"I don't want to transfer. I don't need a four year degree," Jimmy explained.

"What did you have in mind?"

"I want to go to the big island. Surf and get a job shaping boards, maybe eventually have my own shop. I'm shaping now part time. My parents are having cardiac-arrest, but that's what I want to do."

So we made out a list of positives and possible negatives. It included being able to surf whenever he wanted to, maybe sleeping in his car for a while and maybe not finding a job right away. It also included the future: maybe never having a lot of money and having to share an apartment with someone forever.

"But how can I help?"

"You were always honest with us in class. Lots of us couldn't believe that we'd actually found a teacher who respected us. But you did. I guess I just wanted your opinion on this whole crazy idea. Am I nuts?"

"Somebody is going to be shaping those boards and riding those waves. Why not you? Even if it is really hard at first…getting settled, a new and strange place…you know what I mean."

He got up from the chair, smiled and went to the door. "I'll email you if I make it."

"*Not if but when* you make it. You've got nothing to lose. You're young." I smiled back. He gave me a "hang loose" salute with his right hand and was gone.

I have always told students to give their own desires a chance, knowing that few would take the risk, but always hoping they would.

Almost eleven months later I did get that email. He had already gone through many of the negatives on his list like sleeping in his car, but he was a talented shaper and found a job in an established shop. The owner gave him a shed in the yard behind the shop where he could shape his own boards after work and then let him sell them in the shop. He already had a backlog of orders and had developed a father-and-son relationship with the owner, which he had never had with his own father. Yes, he was always scraping for money. Yes, he shared a small house with four other people.

But every time the waves were up, they'd close the shop and ride the big ones. I smiled to myself. Jimmy was making his own history now.

Just Beautiful

As the semesters passed and when the weather was nice, my classes liked sitting outside. The college had a small amphitheater that sat on a high knoll overlooking the yacht harbor and ocean. It was ideal for a class of about thirty. They would gather round and we could conduct class there.

In one of my classes, there was a very open and personable young woman who I thought was truly beautiful. Unlike many students, Carrie did not fear expressing her ideas because they had not been suppressed during her early education and freely gave her opinions and insights. During one class in the sun, she introduced the question of a form of slavery after the end of Reconstruction (1877) when we were talking about the results of the Civil War.

She was writing one of her class papers on the bondage in which Afro-Americans were held after the war. The book she was reading was called *Slavery by Another Name* by Douglas A. Blackmon, and neither I nor the class had ever heard of it or the idea that the form of slavery that took place between 1877 and World War II was far worse in its cruelty and general abuse than original slavery.

I asked her to tell us about it and she immediately launched into a narrative that brought the selling of Afro-Americans by cities and counties to private and public companies to life, keeping them in the worse possible conditions and many times working them to death when their only shortcoming had been a minor crime or a trumped up conviction without evidence. She essentially taught that segment of the class, and it was interesting and certainly illuminating. I thanked her when she was finished, and the class ended.

Afterwards, one of my best male students came up to me and said, "She's hot, and so intelligent."

"Why would that surprise you, Mike? Can't a woman be beautiful and smart too?"

"Oh…well…sure," he momentarily stammered, "But it was just amazing to see someone who could be in the movies talking about history."

"So, we both learned something?"

"Wow, yes." He hesitated. "You think I dare ask her out?"

"Why do you ask?"

"Well, I figure she gets plenty of attention being that beautiful."

"My experience has been that often really beautiful women are sometimes lonely because good men are afraid to ask them out." Mike nodded his head in agreement. "So, what's the harm in trying? All she can say is no."

The expression on his face was hesitant, but turned quickly to a smile. "Okay, I'll give it a try."

"Good, see you next class." As he walked away, I remembered how scared I had always been in the same circumstance. But I always rationalized the situation away and never tried. I hoped Mike wasn't like I had been at his age.

*No one is so wrong as the man
who knows all the answers.*
Chuang Tsu

Summer School Recovery?

In the middle of the spring semester of my third year, the Chairman of the department asked me if I would like to teach the last three weeks of the six-week summer session with him. It was considered an honor and the person chosen was from then on, on good behavior, designated as the most senior part-time instructor in the department. He asked me to sit in so I could see how he "shaped them up" on the first day.

For one living in a coastal city, summer seldom meant hot like the east coast, and the day we began at 8 a.m. (there were two classes, one from 8-10 and the other 10-12 Monday through Thursday) it was almost chilly with a slight breeze off the ocean.

I sat in the first row: the row that often isn't occupied until all other seats are taken, perhaps because students fear being called upon. The students kept filing in well past eight o'clock, probably because they were new to the campus and didn't know where all the buildings were. Or parking was awful as always. Or so I thought.

As those that filed in late arrived, he would make comments like, "Better late than never" or "The late bird never gets the worm." When all appeared to be settled, he stood next to the lectern calling off names and checking them off his roster. When he was through, he paced back and forth with a kind of scowl as he stared out at the students. "A warning; I will grade you just like I would if this was a university. For many of you that will probably mean a C."

He spotted a young girl who sat next to me, but before he spoke to her he addressed the class in general. "No excuse for being late to my classes. I expect you to be here on time and ready to listen and learn the subject. Are there any questions on that matter?"

One student in the middle of the class meekly raised his hand. "Ah, Sir."

"I'm Dr. Olson," he corrected.

"Yes, Dr. Olson, I'm sure you know how hard parking is here during the regular semester. Well, it isn't much better in the summer so it's kind of hard…"

"Please don't whine. Just come to school earlier and you'll be fine. Is that clear?" The student nodded reluctantly. Dr. Olson then directed his attention to the girl next to me who had a cup of coffee on her desk. He slightly glared at her. "Ah, Miss Yuppie Coffee Drinker. The school policy is that no students can bring coffee or any foods into class. Do you know why? Miss Yuppie Coffee, do you know why?" She was almost in tears now, being picked out of the class on the first day, and in the front row.

"Because food or coffee might spill and cause a mess?" she answered.

"Ah, yes. Miss Yuppie already displays brain function. And another reason?

"I…I'm not sure…the expense to the school to get it cleaned up."

"Excellent, so you can take that coffee or whatever it is, and empty it in the sink next door in the women's restroom. We'll anticipate your return."

The girl's pain was moving in my own stomach as she went out the door. "Good. I hope that is clear to all of you?" There were embarrassed nods as she came back in and sat down. I tried to smile at her without his seeing it.

He handed out the syllabus and assignment sheet and forged immediately into the first lecture. He knew his subject well, having taught it for thirty years. There was a rumor among the students that he had been using the same notes and jokes for thirty years. He spoke in a rapid fire fashion, punctuating his remarks with what appeared to be nearly illegible scrolls on the board. He spoke without hesitation, as if he were alone in the room and when a couple students tried to raise their hands, he ignored them. As I left, I tried again to smile at the young girl, but her head was down as if she were hiding.

I would reappear at the beginning of the fourth week and wondered how those forty students had fared in the meantime. He was writing the midterm grades on the board when I entered.

The grades were 0 A's, 6 B's, 25 C's, 6 D's and a few F's. Just before he left he again emphasized that he graded as they would be graded at the university to which they might transfer.

He had barely stepped out the door when I sensed a lot of tension and emotion from the class. It must have been held in check for three weeks. They didn't even know me, except a few by reputation, so their emotions on my first day being so out in the open surprised me.

The first thing I did was smile and say, "Wow!"

Then I went over to the young girl who had been singled out the first day. She was still sitting in the first row. I had my latte with me and I carried it over where she sat. "What's that?" I asked with the hint of a smile.

She returned a small smile as she spoke, "It's coffee or a latte or tea."

"I hate tea." I responded. "But you're right, it is a latte. Everybody see this? We're not supposed to have this or food in class. It's policy, right?

So, my god, I have broken a rule. Everybody listening? If you want to bring a coffee or something to eat, be my guest. I'll have a latte every day, so if a stray administrator happens to wander in, he or she'll catch us all." They laughed and I could feel some of the tension subsiding. I looked at her again. "Okay?" She nodded.

"They don't want us to have any food or drink in here because why?" No one raised their hand or spoke. "It's because they assume we will make a mess. But I have never had a class that brought in food who left a mess. They always put their waste in the basket on the way out, right?"

"Right," they said. A student in the back raised his hand.

"You don't have to raise your hand. If you have something to say, just let it out. I seldom find students interrupting each other except in the heat of a lively discussion. What's your name?" I asked the boy. He was tall and thin, with what looked like it might one day be a real beard, and his nose was pierced.

"Robert, Sir."

"My name is Roger, not Sir or Doctor or Mister or any of that silly stuff. I know, I know, that's how you've been indoctrinated and you can call me anything you want but I prefer my first name." They nodded in unison. "So, Robert, tell me what's up?"

For the next half hour, the unplugging of pent up emotions took over the classroom. Robert told how he had been locked out of the class because he was late, even though it was due to a flat tire.

Then a young woman, almost in tears, spoke up from the third row. "My...my girlfriend walked out crying...and...and she really needed this class to transfer to the university. She just couldn't take his wise cracks anymore. Now she has to go another semester for just one class."

A boy about eighteen spoke cynically and softly, as if he was embarrassed to say what he had to say because he thought I would take it the wrong way. "His midterm sucked. You'd have to be a historian to know the answer to some of the multiple choice questions and his essay was so broad there wasn't time to throw in all the facts. It just wasn't fair. We were all doomed to getting C's." There was a murmur throughout the class. I felt their bitterness. I stood there for a second and looked at them.

"Alright, that's the past. We've got three weeks to go. Don't believe anything I say from this moment on unless you see me do what I say: meaning, I back up my opinions and respect yours. Agreed?" There were many shaking heads, even some high fives in the air. "As for the final, I will give you a choice to take the one he left or a final I write. My final will be three questions. I will give them to you in advance and from your reading and my lectures you should have them answered before you get to the final. On that day, I will tell you which two of the three to write on. Clear?"

I find in-class exams, especially midterms and finals nothing more than an exercise of "in-one-ear-and-out-the-other." Slowly, things began to ease off. You could feel it in the air. More students talked, more got over the stigma of calling me by my first name. I knew most of theirs when summer school ended. What I didn't know was that innocently I had crossed a line that wasn't supposed to be crossed. I had dared to exercise so called "academic freedom." I would soon learn that the "freedom" I had always believed in didn't exist.

Forming a Circle in the Grass After the Attack

When the fall semester began just after the summer school experience, I was leaving the house early for school when the gardener across the street came running over. Judging from his face, it looked like there was a terrible monster loose in the neighborhood.

"Did you hear it? Go back and watch it on TV. Planes crashing into the Twin Towers in New York! We're under attack!"

I went back into the house, thinking this was just some hype by one of the networks to sell soap with the news, but when I turned on the TV there was a split screen and a plane was crashing into each building and enveloping them in flames. The reporters had almost lost it and spoke almost hysterically. Their fearful delivery screamed out of the screen. I watched unbelieving, then called my wife. Neither of us could believe it. What do you do? What could anyone do? It was around nine-thirty in the east, a time when most everyone is already at work. What of the people who were on those floors where the planes crashed? What of the others in the building or in buildings around that part of New York?

I left to walk to the college about five miles away. Everyone I passed seemed to be talking about it, shouting about it to neighbors, even to a passersby like me.

Nothing had changed. The college was as always, alone up on a hill overlooking the Pacific Ocean. The colleagues I passed in the hall on the way to my office had comments that ranged from "The chickens have finally come home to roost" to "Are we under attack?" Otherwise everything in the mail room seemed normal. The sun was already bright. A new college day had begun.

I walked into class and stood in front of my students waiting for everyone to file in and take a seat. There were bewildered looks all around. Some students were talking about the crashes and others asked me if I had heard about it. At that moment, I had no idea what I was going to do that day in my three classes with about fifty students in each.

I looked at them as it grew silent. Suddenly it came to me; I knew what we would do that day. I smiled, raised my arm and said, "Please, come with me." Everyone rose and we walked down the hall to the stairs, out of the building and toward the knoll to our right where we could see a clear, bright, blue sea. We walked to about twenty yards from the edge of the knoll into a large area of freshly cut lawn.

"Let's gather in a circle. I know it will be big, but let's settle down here in the grass."

Lucky for us it wasn't wet and everyone managed to fit in the circle and close it as tight as we could. "Okay, now I want everyone to hold hands and breathe naturally. You can pray, meditate, stare into space, whatever you decide. Let's all just be still and hold hands for the next ten minutes and listen to what's around us."

A bell rung in the distance and the pathways cleared of people as classes began. After ten minutes, I asked if they could feel the mutual energy from hand to hand. Many nodded. "Okay you can keep holding or drop hands, whatever feels right to each of you. Now let's talk about it."

For the next hour we discussed what had happened. Some said they had a relative or family friend who worked in one of the buildings. Some said we should seek revenge on whoever did this awful act. Still others talked about U.S. foreign policy and how our actions historically had resulted in many countries not liking us, and this disaster was a long time coming. There were all types of opinions and debate from the most liberal to the most conservative, and that's how we spent the hour.

I did the same thing with my next two class with similar results. It just seemed that a lecture on previous U.S. history wasn't appropriate because of such an event, which itself was history.

For the next several days, I had students come to my office, talk to me in class or see me around campus. Many relayed how confused they had been about the whole thing. On the day it happened, many weren't even thinking of coming to school. The most general comment was "That circle, holding hands, being quiet for a while and then talking about it made me feel more steady, made me feel we'd get through it together somehow." The next most general comment was that in none of their other classes was it even discussed. I asked several of my colleagues about what the students had told me and they acted surprised that leaving the classroom and the agenda behind for a day was odd, to say the least.

To imagine is everything, to know is nothing at all.

Anatole France

The Chairman's Evaluation

After the summer school class, the department chairman, Al Olson, and I always seemed to get along, even socializing with our wives a couple of times, so I expected this November evaluation to be just like the past ones. He had always given me the highest marks in every category. On one level, I was correct: high marks but with a twist.

He smiled and motioned me to a chair in his office. "How goes it Roger?"

"Very good, Al, no complaints. I'm very happy with all my classes."

He smiled again. "Good. Well, it's evaluation time again and I have a couple things I want to go over with you. Okay?"

"Shoot."

"Everything seems in order, but I still do have some concerns about your teaching style. Oh, I know, you get lots of praise from students. I just received this." He handed me a copy of a note from the college president with a note of praise from not only a student, but also the student's parents. "You can have that copy. Basically it says their kid loves the class and how you related past and present and sprinkle your lectures with personal experience stories." He paused and stared at the papers on his desk. His office could best be described as a running over file cabinet, but he always seemed to know where everything was and he was very dedicated to his work.

He continued, "My concern is twofold. I want to make sure you are giving the students enough real history in your lectures, and I would suggest that you get the media department to video one of your lectures so you can evaluate how you are doing. You know the habit you have of holding your lecture notes as you walk back and forth, and even up the aisles? You've got to keep letting them know who is boss. Getting familiar with them by walking the aisles does distract from your authority. Also, carrying your notes gives the impression that you don't know your subject very well."

"Al, the reason I sometimes walk up and down the aisles is to be personal, to let them know that I'm not just a figure standing at a lectern in front of them. I think softening the authority figure helps. At least I find it that way. And carrying notes is because I sometimes forget things and I don't want to run back to the lectern every time I do."

Al shook his head vigorously. "I know, I know and I can't argue with your statistics. The dean was telling me a few days ago that you had the highest retention rate of any part or full time instructor in the school again last semester, but I still think the video would be good and I'd like you to visit Johnson's class. He's over in Building D207 Tuesday and Thursday at eleven. That should work for you?" I nodded. "What I'm concerned about is that you need to put more history into your lectures and I think Johnson, he's a Ph.D. candidate at the university, will give you a good example of that. Well, that's it for now. Any questions?"

"Yes. I don't see the student written evaluations in this package. I always like to look at those."

"Oh, I guess I forgot them. Let me see." He poked around his massively littered desk and handed me some papers on which the department secretary had typed the student comments.

Later, I read these. There were nine single spaced pages and 95% of them were complimentary. They ranged from "Good teacher" to "I hate history, but I really liked this class and learned a lot."

As I walked home that day, I had a deep, intuitive sense that somehow I wasn't the senior adjunct or fair-haired boy anymore.

The Recommended Example

I got to Mr. Johnson's class a few minutes early and explained that the chairman had recommended I sit in on his class to pick up some pointers. He said that was fine with him and I sat down in the second row as the other students filed in and stared at me as they took seats. By the time they were seated, only a handful chose the front row.

Johnson immediately began calling the roll. With his head bent over the lectern and reading the roll sheet, he never looked up to place a name with a face. When he finished, he did look up as if to ask if there were questions, but his eyes rotated back and forth against the back wall of the room over the students' heads.

Dr. Olson had been right. Mr. Johnson really poured on the history, facts and dates, but there was never any discussion of the issues these facts and dates raised or any relevance to modern times, of which I found many. For a full forty-five minutes, his eyes never left their rotation against the back wall until he had finished lecturing. Only then did he nod at the students, pick up his notes and depart. I shook his hand and thanked him for his time.

As he walked briskly away from the classroom, I couldn't help but wonder what he thought he had taught and whether the students believed they had learned anything. Also, if Dr. Olson had recommended him, was I supposed to believe this was the kind of teaching that was considered the general example for everyone to follow?

I realized that Dr. Olson, without saying it, had put me on my guard. I would only know just how much on my guard when he handed out the course assignments for the spring semester a week later.

*Our eyes were originally right, but
went wrong because of teachers.*

Ah-eng Ku

The Race Card and Vietnam

I was teaching a terrific night class from 6 to 9 p.m. I never liked teaching at night but it did help the income, being the third class, a maximum for part time teachers. I have always felt that people who go to school at night after an eight hour work day are the most courageous students.

On the first night I told them that.

It was a diverse class with people from all ages and backgrounds, seventeen to sixty, waiters to accountants and business managers. For the most part, they were a dream because they participated actively and were not timid about giving their opinion, liberal or conservative, and they kept me inspired all semester. Perhaps the highlight of all was a presentation by a Vietnam veteran who I had asked to tell us about his impressions and experiences in that controversial war. But before his heartfelt, emotional talk, I have another experience from that term to share.

One night I was a little late, but earlier than most of my students. The building in which I taught had classes without windows and, on the other side of the hall, classes with windows. Mine had windows. As I was about to enter, I noticed a couple dozen students sitting on the floor outside. I asked them why they couldn't get into the room and they said it was locked and they were waiting for their teacher to open it.

One student asked me, "How long do we have to wait for the teacher to show up? Last week he was ten minutes late."

"If it were me, I would wait twenty minutes and take off." I told them my name and department in case they had any problems.

As I was opening my door, one student said, "He didn't show up a couple weeks ago at all."

This was odd because the class, three units, only met one night a week: that was it. "Well, as I said, you have my name and I'll be your witness if you get in any trouble."

Soon my class had assembled and I was caught up in the beginning of a discussion and lecture on Globalization. Twenty minutes passed and I heard the students across the hall exiting the building. I opened the door and one student motioned that their teacher had not shown up, again. I re-entered my room and we began a discussion on the material we'd just talked about.

The next day I stopped by the office of the chairman of the Latino Studies Program. We had known each other for five years. "You got a minute?"

He motioned me to sit. He was a quiet, slightly balding man who looked Anglo but was Mexican. "What's up?"

"This Dr. Palama who teaches the night Latino Studies class across the hall from mine. It's about him."

He shook his head and looked for a long moment at me. "We've been trying for five years to get rid of him without success. He's had three formal academic reviews. What happened this time?"

"His students tell me he's missed at least two night classes. I've also heard from a former student of mine who took a class from him that he sometimes forgets to grade or correct papers and returns them unmarked. How does somebody like that get to stay on?"

"He has tenure and it's almost impossible to fire someone with tenure unless they practically rape or kill a student." As an afterthought he said, "And he's Mexican like me, which as you must know is a plus for him."

"Juan, you know what I think. A guy like that shows no respect for himself or his students."

Juan nodded. "Would you write me a letter describing what you saw? I can send it up to the Dean."

I wrote the letter and he turned it in to the Dean the next day. I was completely surprised by the reaction of some of my colleagues. They charged me with breaking ranks and said things like "You never side with the administration. We stick together." I told them I didn't buy that when it hurt our students. In fact, Dr. Palama confronted me a week later in the mail room.

"You could have come to me."

"Look, don't lay your shortcomings on me. It was you who caused this to happen and you're the one who needs to accept the blame." After that, some colleagues began avoiding me.

The semester continued and I was caught up in my work though I didn't fail to notice that two more times Dr. Palama did not show up.

By this time in the semester, we were talking about Vietnam. The war had been over for about three decades and my night class had many people in it who had gone through the war. Those that were older had vivid memories of protests and National Guardsmen firing into student crowds in places like Kent State University, Ohio. Even the most conservative among them understood the very wrongness of this war, but that discussion paled in light of what my Vietnam veteran had to say.

He was about fifty-five, tall and a little stout, as men get at that age, and his eyes, at least to me, were the eyes of an innocent, not a combat veteran. He began to speak and a silence I had never felt in a class followed. It felt as deep as the silence of a forest, miles from civilization. It was as if all of us had come to a stop.

"I was at a Marine fire base. It was built on high ground and really the only practical way in or out was by chopper because the one road was mined by the Cong. We had killed all the vegetation for two hundred yards and erected, at the cost of quite a few lives, a maze of mines and barbed wire to prevent entry. Yet that didn't stop the mortars, machine gun and rifle fire that hit us sporadically during the day and night. Our job was to go out into the jungle and find and kill Cong or bring them in for interrogation. I had signed up for the Marines with a high school buddy. We were in a program where we would always go to the same place, and we ended up there at the fire base.

"Daily casualties were the norm because when you are walking around a compound taking off-and-on fire day and night you have to be pretty thick skinned not to feel the fear that the next one might be yours. A couple times at night they even managed to hit one of the bunkers where we were dug in to sleep, eat and just lounge, if you can call it that." He tried to smile and make light of it, but his face wouldn't move into a smile.

"You've heard the saying 'war is hell.' Well, believe me, it was. Patrols were bad enough but then coming back to a place that could also get you killed doubled the fear. In reality, you just couldn't relax the whole tour of duty there. There was fear all the time, but we seldom talked about it. We were supposed to be Marines, afraid of nothing.

"It…" His mouth quivered suddenly and tears poured without shame down his face. I could see that it startled the class, none of whom had had such an experience. It felt like what he was about to share was as real as the moment. He was back at that fire base. "I was…coming back from a patrol. It was just before sunset in the spring so the Vietnam sky looked like a crowd of orange clouds. We had just made the last turn into the so called safe ground just below the base itself. I could see up the hill and across the compound to the other side. My high school buddy was there and we waved. I was glad to be back, even to that hole." He shifted his vision to his feet.

"Then…then…" He was trying to keep back the tears but they flowed even more. "Then I heard this clap of thunder. That's how a mortar sounds hitting the earth, shaking the hell out of everything. When I looked up, I saw nothing but smoke. My…my buddy was gone."

He wiped his eyes and blew his nose. Some composure was trying to return. "We…were…we were out of there in about a month, going home." He was suddenly silent, staring out at the class. No one took their eyes off of him. Then he said, "That was my 'Nam experience."

The class had run over ten minutes, but no one had shown the usual restlessness. Slowly they got up and approached the Vet. His hands were still on the lectern. One of the younger students awkwardly reached out and hugged him, then others followed. At least three-fourths of the class hugged and thanked him.

When they left, I finally spoke. "Telling that story, Ted, took incredible courage. Thank you." And I hugged him as we left the room together.

I didn't run into the Vet for a couple of years, but when I did he told me he was doing much better and his wife confirmed that. He was managing an elder care center. As for Dr. Palama, well he's still teaching at the college. As for me, I was about to receive an incredible gift from my students.

The Petition

The spring class assignments were in my mailbox. I had been reduced from three classes to two by Dr. Olson. The scribbled note merely said, "Making room for more part timers." But I knew it was more than that.

At dinner I talked it over with my wife. "That hurts a little financially, but we'll get by." I knew she was, as always, just putting on a brave face. "You probably should have used his damned summer school final and this may not have happened." I was about to interrupt and tell her that over 90% of the students had opted for my final exam instead of his but she cut me off. "Yes, I know, you probably have one of the highest student evaluations of any teacher in the school, but that doesn't seem to count much with Dr. Olson."

"I told you how the summer school class was. I had no choice but to try and salvage my three weeks."

The next day the one close acquaintance I had made in my five years of teaching at the college nearly echoed my wife. He shook his head and reminded, "You know what happens when you get on his bad side."

"But I thought the last three weeks were mine to teach the subject as I saw fit. Academic freedom, you know?"

He smiled and shook his head again. "Roger, my boy, I'm a philosopher and you're a dreamer. Wasn't it Machiavelli who said unarmed prophets always lose? You just disarmed the hell out of yourself by not doing it his way. He's the Prince, don't you know that?"

"Yeah, last summer one of my so-called colleagues who taught another summer class with him thought his exams were as bad as I did but she copped out by asking him if she could just change a few of the multiple choice questions."

"I know, my lad, but she still has her three classes next semester."

The fall semester was soon over and I taught the two classes in the spring. I was able to increase enrollment to make up some of the pay I had lost and also help some students who would have had to wait another semester to take the course.

About halfway through the semester a student asked why I didn't have three classes. I was not honest with him and said only that I had only been given two to make room for more part timers. "Yeah, but you've been here a while haven't you? Hasn't it always been three? I was recommended to you by a couple of friends." All I could do was nod.

Over the next few weeks, former and current students would see me on campus and showed me copies of notes and letters they had sent to the Dean of Social Sciences and the college President who himself had called me in to discuss letters of praise from students and parents that he had received. They also sent one to the school newspaper which did a small but weak story on my situation.

The semester was coming to a close and again in my mailbox was my course assignment for the fall. I had been cut to one class by Dr. Olson. I was mad and soon confronted him in the mail room, asking, "Why have you taken my livelihood and love away?" He left not bothering to answer.

Two weeks before the semester was over, a student in my second class showed up at my first class and asked if I would step outside for a minute because he wanted to talk to the class. I waited outside and after about ten minutes he came out, smiled a "thank you" and left. He would do the same thing in the other class an hour and a half later.

I didn't find out what he was up to until we talked just before summer started.

"I submitted a petition signed by every student in both of the class sections you taught this semester to the Dean and the President." I was so overcome that I thanked and hugged him. "Now we'll see whether these assholes have any integrity." He transferred to a university that term and I never saw him again, but I was immensely proud that he had been my student. I had no idea where this would all go, but it wouldn't be long before it all became very obvious.

The Exit Interview

Summer began with a trip east to the Ivy League graduation of my daughter. We combined the trip with a beautiful drive up the New England coast and a three-day stay on Nantucket Island before returning home.

I wasn't home a week when I got a call from my Dean, asking me to come and see him and the Vice President in two days. I was joyous because I felt my students' petition had paid off and I was being considered for one or two more classes.

"Come on in, Roger," the Vice President invited, "The Dean and I wanted to talk to you about the fall semester. As you know, Dr. Olson has cut you to one class."

"And he cut me from three to two this last semester," I added. They both nodded. I got the feeling they were embarrassed.

"Roger," the vice president continued, "Your record since you've been here is as good as it gets. Nobody could have a better retention rate or student and chair evaluations." He looked at the Dean as if for support.

"Dr. Olson wants to discontinue you, so you won't have any classes next semester." I must have looked shocked because the Dean interjected quickly. "Our hands are really tied because he is the Department Chair and we must defer to him."

"But what about my record?"

"We agree and can only say how sorry we are that this has happened. But Dr. Olson did submit some material, a blue book by one of your former students. You gave him a B in the class, yet we have both read his essay and think it is barely worth a C."

"May I see it?" The Dean pulled it from a folder and I examined it. I looked at both of them, "I never taught this class and this isn't one of my students." They didn't have a reply for a moment.

"Dr. Olson said it was one of your former students. Are you sure he is mistaken?" I nodded. "Then we're sorry about that. Dr. Olson thinks you pander to your students and are too easy on them."

"Dr. Olson himself once read a couple of exams I graded. He actually said I was too hard on my students, and as far as pandering, if treating my students with respect, something I don't remember too often in twenty-five years in school, then, yes, I pander to them. Just for your information I poll my classes each semester and ask them two questions. First, 'How many teachers could you really talk to as people, not just in their roles of student and teacher?' Their answer is consistently three or four. Then I ask them 'How many could you trust?' and their answer is always a thumb and first finger held in the shape of a zero. If that's not a condemnation of the way they've been taught, I don't know what is." I sighed. "Okay, let's not prolong this. Thanks for calling me in and telling me." I got up and shook hands with each of them. Then I turned and left.

How could I ever have thought student support would be taken seriously? How naïve I was to think that a student petition and a school newspaper article would influence administrators.

My Supporters?

This will be a very short story.

When Dr. Olson was cutting me to just one class, there was nothing I could do. As an adjunct instructor, my union too was powerless. I had nowhere to turn.

When I asked the Dean and Vice President if they had talked to any of my colleagues, they said they had and they had all sided with Dr. Olson.

One of them who would soon abandon me, though my wife and I had many dinners with him over the years, was someone I thought had integrity based upon his own bumpy life. He said, "You never go up against a thirty-year tenured professor. Never."

"I thought it was all about students, not different opinions on how to teach them?"

He smiled. "My friend, you just learned reality the hard way." I remembered many stimulating and humorous conversations we had shared, but this would be our last. He never called us again.

The administrators also told me that the Latino Studies Chairman, who had told me he would try to support me, just kept silent and offered no defense to Dr. Olson or the administrators even though he had attended my class and gave an excellent report of it.

A professor from another department told me, sourly, when he heard of the student petition, "I don't like things like that. Teachers should not encourage students in that way." I told him my students had initiated the petition not me but he refused to believe that, as if they actually lacked the ability to create such an action.

And finally, the one woman, the only woman, in the department who had always praised me when I substituted for her, actually supported Dr. Olson. She was a tenured professor who had nothing to lose by supporting me. Consistently, she would tell me how much her classes enjoyed the lecture or lectures I had given them when she had asked me to substitute for her.

I had always revered the academic world as a place where ideas were welcome and ideals were defended.

I knew this was the end of my academic career in my home town.

The alternatives were either thirty-five miles south, and I had no desire to drive any closer to Los Angeles, or eighty miles north to a community that was very much based in an agricultural culture. Either way, there was no guarantee I would find work, especially with the stigma of being "discontinued" from my previous job. I decided to apply north and sent an email to the Chairman of Social Sciences along with a summary of my work, including student comments and my overall ranking as a teacher in the school. The same day I received an email back from a man whose tone I instantly liked. He invited me up for lunch and offered me one night class beginning in the fall.

Though I hated the waste of gas and wear and tear on my car, I loved teaching more. My new career was launched again in less than a year.

I think we need a **FIVE MINUTE BREAK TO RING THE TEMPLE BELL** *so I can include a couple vignettes that have nothing to do with my teaching but are both truly educational. The first is a story a high school teacher told me and the second is a story from a jazz trumpeter.*

Joe Wood's Class: The Kid in the Hoody

Joe had done an around the world surfing tour before he decided to go back to school and become a teacher. His problem at the beginning was that all his savings had gone to riding waves, so he worked as an undergraduate. He married a graduate student and as luck would have it, his wife had a real job that helped him focus on his teaching credential and graduate with honors.

By his third year of teaching, the marriage had fallen apart, but he always tried to keep that out of his classroom. He had also incurred the jealousy of many of his Humanities Department colleagues because he was easily the most sought after teacher, not just in the department but also the school. Why?

It was pretty obvious to anyone who ventured into his classroom; he respected his students in a way that most teachers just don't seem to. This was an English classroom, but the walls not only displayed the poems and songs written by his students, past and present, but their art work and photography as well. This was a room filled with student pride that was always promoted by their teacher.

You could drop by any lunch period and the room would be full of students talking to Joe, playing a game on the class computer or just hanging out on the couch he managed to bring in with opposition from some administrators. The miracle was that most of these students didn't even have a class after lunch with Joe, they just migrated there because it felt like a home.

Once when we were eating lunch at his desk he told me a story I would never forget because it equals everything great about teaching and a teacher who wasn't afraid to teach honestly.

The year before, Joe was teaching a class of seniors. He taught a high school college-prep class, one step below Advanced Placement students. For the first three weeks a tall, lean boy with a mop of uncombed black hair would come in, sit in the very back, and keep his head buried under his hoody and between his arms for the whole class period.

One of the really bright girls who should have been in AP classes but said she didn't like all the competition that went on there, asked Joe a zinger of a question, one that teachers are often told is too personal and definitely shouldn't be answered. The class was talking about a short story they had just read about a woman who had gotten a divorce. "Woods?" (all his students called him that) the girl asked, "You got divorced a while ago. What's it like?"

Joe had stood silent for a moment debating whether he should or shouldn't and, being Joe, he decided he should. For the rest of the class period he talked, from his perspective, about the anger, the hate, the fear, and the loss that had made up his own painful divorce. In fact, he really wasn't over it, even after eight months.

They asked a lot of questions and he answered them all, even the ones that still hurt. The class ended with their thanking him for talking about it and they filed out. The lean kid in the hoody stopped at his desk and waited for everyone else to leave. Then he spoke.

"That…that really meant…well it meant a lot to me." Suddenly it looked like the boy had a tear in one eye and his face had grown bright red. "You see…that's what I'm going through right now with my parents and it meant a lot to hear it from you."

Joe grabbed the boy gently by the shoulders. "Write about it and let me read it. I'll make it one of the assignments you've already missed." The boy brushed another tear and nodded, quickly exiting the class.

The next class he turned in a ten page, typewritten paper. It was very personal and also well written and organized. Joe was knocked flat by the honesty and insight the boy was able to communicate.

After that, everything changed. The boy didn't wear the hood anymore or put his head down. He actually bought a notebook, took notes and turned in the rest of the assignments as they came due. He managed a B+ for the class.

The next semester, Joe was brought up on sexual harassment charges by his colleagues. There was not a shred of evidence. They couldn't even produce a witness, and with the union's help he was returned in good standing to his class to continue to teach. Joe is still teaching, still working his magic and still reaching his students in his own unique way.

The other story is about another unique teacher who played jazz trumpet and read a whole lot of philosophy. Though he gave me a greater appreciation for the art of thinking, he also taught me about the art of the possible, the art of being.

> *In a society where competition for the basic cultural goods is a pivot of action, people cannot be taught to love one another. It thus becomes necessary for the school to teach children to hate and without appearing to do so, for our culture cannot tolerate the idea that babes should hate each other.*
>
> R.D. Laing

Playing Jazz Trumpet and Reading Philosophy

Dr. Rashid Amalli sat in his office on the second floor of the administration building. He had a view of the campus from there which stretched along flower beds and perfectly tended lawns and cement pathways. Ten o'clock classes were just over and students and professors crisscrossed the campus.

It was hard to know what to say when a student is bent on leaving the security of a small college that was slowly becoming elite in both student and faculty choices. Conservative, becoming hypercompetitive and pro-business, the new President was rapidly building an impressive endowment fund that had grown more in the last two years than the previous twenty. Dr. Amalli perceived the handwriting on the wall but ignored it as he waited for Ed Johnson, a student from both a divorced and poor family.

Ed knocked on the always open door and Dr. Amalli motioned him in with a smile. As Dean of Students, he seldom had appointments where someone wanted to leave the school.

"Hey, Ed. Sit down."

Ed sat slowly down in one of the two straight leather chairs across the desk from Dr. Amalli. Every other Dean already had brand new ultra-modern office furniture, but Dr. Amalli was still waiting.

"So, what can I do for you, Ed?"

"I just wanted your opinion on my wanting to leave this place."

Dr. Amalli nodded. "Why would a class officer like you—your peers obviously respect you—want to leave mid-year…or ever?"

"I…I just feel out of place here. I don't have any real friends except Dick Bill and he's considered an odd ball by most of my classmates."

"How so?"

"He's just wandering. Never studies…and when he does it's the night before an exam…and somehow he always comes out okay, despite never going to class."

Dr. Amalli leaned forward. "But this is about you?"

"Yeah," Ed looked over his shoulder for a moment and stared out the window. "I don't know exactly what it is but most of my teachers act like they don't give a damn what any of us say. It's all about what they think. And I'm tired of the race for grades. It's bullshit."

"I can understand how you could feel that way, but is that why you want to leave?"

"That and all the college phoniness. Like you're considered disloyal if you don't attend team events. Stuff like that. I just want to go somewhere where I can get lost a little bit. Somewhere I'm not forced on people like here."

"Where?"

"Berkeley."

Dr. Amalli smiled. "You can really get lost there. Twenty-two thousand students." He shifted in his chair. "You're a junior. I won't blame you if you can't answer this, but do you have any idea what you want to do?"

"I want to be a writer. I know that's far out and so called impractical but that's it."

"You've written for our literary magazine haven't you?"

"Yeah, and some little magazine just accepted one of my short stories."

"Let me tell you a little story. It may or may not answer your question, which I'm sure also is asked because you have doubts."

"Right, more than you think. I wouldn't have a scholarship there and my family is dead set against me going."

"Ed, when I was your age I was playing jazz trumpet in dives in Chicago."

"You're kidding?"

"No, it's true. It was a rough time. In a couple of cases I saw people gunned down, gang style, during a set. We'd get mob types who would keep putting hundred dollar bills on the piano and telling our piano man that they liked waltzes. So that's what we played, or whatever they wanted.

"Anyway, I was about twenty-six when I realized that I was tired of eating dinner at three in the morning and sleeping 'til noon. I'd been reading philosophy since I was nineteen on my own. I'd read all the major thinkers by then. One day—and please don't spread this around."

Ed nodded.

"One day the whole thing came to a head. I'd been semi-depressed for weeks. I just felt like I didn't have any direction, anywhere to go but the next club. I honestly contemplated taking my own life."

"You're really kidding now, right?"

Dr. Amalli shook his head. "Luckily, I had to go to work. By the time I got home, I just lay awake all night. That morning I called one of my friends in the jazz group who respected my work with the horn and I confessed my feeling. We met for lunch and he asked me about all the reading I had done. Had I thought of teaching philosophy? That was when it first hit me. It scared me. I didn't know. But after a few weeks the idea sounded better. Yet I had no idea how I could get into school. I had no formal education, just a high school degree.

"I knew I didn't want to stay in Chicago, and with the little money I saved I moved out here where it was at least warmer. I had no clue. I checked out the jazz scene and it was minimal. I had to do something to support myself if, and it was a big if, I ever got into college. I had no skills other than music, so I applied for the post office. They were short on people for some reason and I got hired working a swing shift. I was living in a marginal neighborhood a couple of miles walk from UCLA, so I figured, what the heck, I'd start there.

"I was naïve. I went directly to the Dean of Education's office, that's how crazy I was. Anyway, to make a long story short, he actually saw me, probably because I was older. He told me they had a special program for older people going back to school which counted their experience. When I told him I wanted to teach philosophy, he smiled and pulled out a newspaper clipping from his desk and had me read it. It said there was an overabundance of teachers."

Dr. Amalli paused. "Don't you see, Ed, this guy just didn't get it. I wanted to teach, period. I didn't care what the market was for teachers.

So I thanked him and got the information how to apply for this special program. I took a battery of tests which included a philosophy exam and got high marks on all of them. They put me in as a senior. When I finished, I was near the top of my class and applied for their Ph.D. program and got in. When I finished, I read the teaching magazines; a job here was advertised. No one seemed to want it because the pay was so bad and this school wasn't considered much back then, but I applied and got the job. As I said, the school was new and not distinguished. I eventually got this job along with my teaching."

Ed smiled for the first time. "Wow."

"Was I just lucky? I don't know."

They were silent for a moment. "Look Ed, an obscure philosopher once said 'Go with your destiny and it will carry you.' Do you understand?"

"Yes." Ed stood up and reached across the desk. They shook hands. "I really appreciate this."

When Ed was gone, Dr. Amalli sat quietly staring out the window and thought about his own future. He knew it was just a matter of time before his degree from UCLA and no real publications would come up now that the college was attracting such "high-powered" faculty.

Where would he go? He sat there until his secretary came to the door and said she was going to lunch. When she was gone he continued to sit until a small smile appeared on his face. There was a teaching job at a new local junior college. He might as well apply before the options on his destiny grew smaller.

He not only got the job, a brand new job at a brand new college in the far eastern part of L.A., but he became the first Chairman of the Philosophy department there. He was doing what he loved in a place where he could do it his way.

Audi

Audi was in a big class, maybe fifty or sixty students, in what I had always thought of as "The Room from Hell." Only a devil could have designed such a room. It was rectangular in shape so there was no way you could have any real conversation with students on either side. The computer stand and projector were in the center, which made it difficult for those on the far sides to see the wall screen. The ceiling was twenty feet high and there were no windows: blank, beige walls only. The only view of the world was an emergency back door that I kept open except in the coldest weather.

Audi, I would learn, was a foster child who joined the Air Force out of high school in order to 1) serve her country and 2) get a down payment on a beyond high school education. She had found Jesus and worked at a local evangelical church in this agricultural community, helping to convince teen and pre-teen girls to abstain from sex until they were married. This she was trying to passionately accomplish in a community that, as I mentioned before, has one of the highest teen pregnancy rates per capita in the United States.

She had already served two tours of duty in Iraq when the conflict there was just forming. Her job was loading bombs onto fighter jets. She had witnessed the tent next to hers destroyed by a rebel rocket. Six of her friends had been sleeping inside and all died instantly.

Unlike most students who have had the fear of ridicule take their voice by the third grade, Audi talked whenever she had a mind to do so. Sometimes she would quote scripture, especially if the lecture touched on controversial subjects. There were always raised eyebrows, but by the middle of the semester I had done what I always have done: give students respect and ask them in turn to give it to each other regardless of what someone says for the simple reason that the person may be sharing something none of us have ever heard before.

For no special reason, she would stop by the front desk sometimes to discuss something from the class that day or tell me how she was making out in a west central coast town far from her Nebraska homeland.

"I just got three new girls in my group," she'd smile proudly. "They've taken the abstinence pledge and they are all strong women, not weaklings. Every week there are new ones!"

"I'm happy for you. Keep it up." I was not against sex before marriage but encouraged her because of her deep sincerity.

At one point, we were reading historian Howard Zinn's book *Passionate Declarations*. The chapter that Audi had just read factually criticized our war efforts historically. This pushed the wrong buttons of a patriotic fundamentalist, and after class she came up shaking the book at me.

"This is a hate book!" she exclaimed.

"How is that, Audi?"

"It's…it's almost communist the way it criticizes this country. It's awful. I don't understand how you could have assigned a book like this."

"I assigned it because it's designed to make you think in ways you've never thought before. And it's written by a man of real integrity and character. I know you appreciate integrity and character. Look at the girls you are working with." She grudgingly shook her head and frowned. "Please, do me the favor of continuing to read. You may surprise yourself."

That's just what Audi did, and she continued to speak out. Though there were still some raised eyebrows, the class overall was taking her and their fellow students more seriously as the semester progressed. She always kept me on my toes. One of many examples of this was when we were discussing the destruction of the environment and the difference between the Indian view of Nature and the colonists' view.

Audi responded "This stuff is just liberal phonies talking. The Bible doesn't say anything about treasuring the environment. When Jesus comes again, the good people will be leaving this planet for a better place anyway." Or another time when she cited the Bible as anti-homosexual.

So often neither I nor the class had answers for her, but a friend on the east coast was a minister and I would email him for help. He always delivered, being a Ph.D. in theology and knowing the Bible backwards and forwards, using it every Sunday in the sermons at his church. He would give me a passage or two and I would offer them to her the next period. Sometimes she would grunt and other times she asked me for the location of a quote I had given her. Most of the time the subject would die and we would continue on, many times with her objections to something I said in lecture or she encountered in one of the books I had assigned.

Liking the assignment or not, Audi always turned in her work on time. For someone who was the product of the U.S. high school system, she was a good writer and her work was clear and organized.

I never give final exams or mid-terms, but we do have a final meeting when the last paper is returned to the students with a grade, along with their final grade, so they don't go into semester break or summer with that anxiety of not knowing. On that final day, Audi came up, the last one to file out with a good-bye, and she stopped to thank me for the A which she had earned and to tell me something I was both surprised and happy to hear.

"You know that Zinn guy? I didn't like him much at first. Still don't in some ways. But I learned some things I never thought about from him and the class in general. Thanks."

"You're not becoming a liberal are you?" She laughed and shook her head.

"Can I ask a favor?" I nodded.

"I'm going back for a third tour in Iraq this summer. My National Guard unit is being deployed again. Could I drop you an email from time to time?"

"Audi, I'd be honored."

She turned and walked out. That was the last I saw her on campus. I am still hoping and waiting for an email.

If all through school the young were provoked to question the Ten Commandments, the sanctity of revealed religion, the foundation of patriotism, the profit motive, the two-party system, monogamy, the laws of incest, and so on, we would have more creativity than we could handle.
Jules Henry

Sophie and the Preacher

In the next semester, there was a young woman with one of the most open and sharp minds I have ever encountered. She would later make a confession she thought was startling, but it just made me smile.

As I watched the students file in the first day, I shuttered at being in another "non-teaching" environment. It was a difficult room without windows or even an outside door. One student caught my eye because he was older, probably sixty-five, with a beard that had lots of gray. He had a fairly good-sized stomach, Nordic complexion and radiant blue eyes. The first day he sat in the front row and remained there for the semester, attending every day and definitely engaged.

She also sat in the front row, directly in front of me and next to the man with the beard. She was Afro-American with an unashamed smile and an alert posture. His name was Bud and hers was Sophie. They were the first two names in a class of forty that I learned because they often participated. From the first lecture, I understood that Bud wanted everyone to know who he was and that he'd read a lot of U.S. history.

After an introduction, we began with the land bridge from Asia as a migration point across the Bering Strait to El Norte, later called the United States and Canada. I had just begun to talk about it when Bud started to raise his hand, then realized he didn't have to do so. "Ah, Roger, it's my understanding that this really was a bridge caused by the Ice Age, when the ocean waters gathered into glaciers to open and expose the land. My question is how long was it open and how many so-called Indians came across from Asia?"

"Well, Bud, it was really more than a bridge. It was actually a huge piece of land and..."

"Sir, ah, Roger?" Sophie stopped me with her smile.

"Yes?"

Bud glanced at her as if she was interrupting his train of thought. There was just the edge of a scowl to it.

"Wasn't it more like a continent because it was over a thousand miles across and the migrants actually lived there for a long time, surviving off the sea and large mammals?"

Bud jumped in. "Where did you get a crazy idea like that? It was a bridge, wasn't it Roger?"

"Sophie is right. The inhabitants remained there for many years until the ice began to melt again and the waters rose." Bud looked suspiciously at Sophie, who just smiled, but not in an 'I told you so' manner. There was confidence in her look.

And that was how the semester passed, a kind of tug-of-war on his side and just an unabashed display of knowledge on her part. Midway through the course Bud asked if he could contribute to the lecture that covered part of Western Expansion, mainly the overland exploration of

Lewis and Clark. He had a special series of maps and presented a slide show, but not without Sophie irritating him with questions about the Indians and the fact that the Lewis and Clark party were not always nice to the Indians, something that had often been left out of textbooks, among other things.

The course only went to 1877, the end of Reconstruction of the north and south after the Civil War, and it was three weeks until the end when Sophie asked for equal time to present a report on her ancestors who had led the way in a white man's world to emancipate the slaves. She was more than fully prepared and her report with slides and quotes from these famous people, along with a good dose of criticism of the North's part in emancipation, managed to do what I always tried: to get the interest of a lot of students who couldn't care less about their history and were just in class to get three transfer credits.

During the whole presentation, Bud was silent and though he had had years of experience speaking before congregations as their minister, Sophie far outshined him. It was plain as day on his face during the whole presentation.

Sophie had already told me she was taking my course for advanced high school credit and I was amazed at how well she presented the material without jitters or nervous swallows or sentences that had "Um" as every third word. It was a magnificent performance. This young girl displayed not the slightest bit of ego and was truly genuine.

She lingered after class and I praised her effort. I happened to mention that I had written some short stories, and she wanted to read them and, if they worked for her, use them the next semester when she was teaching a creative writing class at her high school, which really surprised me. When we walked out, all the students and Bud had gone, she paused.

"May I tell you something?"

"Sure, anything"

She smiled that youthful smile full of both innocence and savvy. "I've been wanting to tell you this for a long time but didn't know how you would take it." She was almost apologizing for what she was about to say.

"Go ahead, tell me. I don't bite."

"Well, you see…I'm fourteen."

This time I smiled. "Sophie this may be college, but your age means absolutely nothing to me. You're not just smart but bright as well and few students are that, even though they all have the potential. I'm just glad you're here."

"I guess Mr. Bud isn't so glad."

"He's just an old guy who falsely thinks he has to prove himself. You'll never be that way."

"Thank you."

After she had gone, I continued to stand there and smile. The rest of the semester Bud was silent, but Sophie kept contributing. I gave her some stories and a few weeks after school she emailed me that she wanted to read some more because she really liked them and wanted to use them in her class.

We lost touch after that. But I know she is still out there continuing to surprise those teachers who are not frightened by her display of knowledge and her confident smile.

Ronald Reagan: The Greatest Socialist President in History

Teaching history in a partially front to back manner gives students a chance to see the results of what came before, so by the time we reached President Reagan we had already seen the perpetuation of the errors of those who came after him.

Manuel was a thinking conservative. He believed in capitalism and all its ramifications, but was open to new ideas and was also someone not afraid to say what he believed. When we got to Mr. Reagan and I explained his history to the class, I asked them, for thought and discussion, whether he was or was not the greatest socialist president in our history, a claim by one of the country's few real economists. Manuel's mouth dropped open and his eyes bugged out slightly. Such a proclamation was like burning the American flag.

Finally, he was able to speak. "How can that be? Reagan was a supply-side economics thinker who believed in democracy and capitalism."

"What is socialism, Juan?"

"It's the redistribution of wealth. Reagan was never for that."

"Yet he transferred over three trillion dollars from the poor and middle class, in the form of entitlement cuts and payroll taxes, as only two examples, to the rich and corporations through tax breaks and loopholes. Isn't that a redistribution of wealth, just like it would be if the wealth had been redistributed from the rich to the poor and middle class?"

Manuel's face seemed to tense up and he immediately wrote something in the computer in which he typed his class notes. It was almost an excuse for not responding.

"And you say he was for democracy, yet he almost single-handedly ruined the union movement when he fired the federal air traffic controllers, which reduced the ability to strike, a key to workers gaining rights, since they fought and died across this country in strikes from almost the beginning of our colonial history, specifically in the late 1800s into the early 1900s. Unions have had their faults, but do you think reducing or eliminating a worker's right to bargain with their employer is democratic?"

We then went on to discuss many of the myths of the Reagan administration. During the rest of the class, Manuel, who usually spoke up, said nothing and left as soon as we were through.

The next day I saw him in the student union when I was getting a coffee. "Well, were the things I suggested without basis in fact?"

"When I told my very conservative friends they thought you were a communist." He paused and looked around him. "But I defended you because I looked that stuff up." I nodded. "But they still wouldn't believe it."

"That's why it's a free country. Even if we have our flaws."

"It's too hard to believe."

"That's okay. Remember what I said on the first day of class: if I don't do or prove what I say, I'm just another phony." He smiled and we parted. Manuel was an excellent listener and learner and I could only hope that I had been balanced in my presentation.

My next class was all the way across campus in a modular building, like a trailer, but unlike many buildings on campus it had the luxury of hot water in the bathrooms, something that was becoming rarer by the year. I was anxious to hear the end of the class that preceded mine because what I had heard so far was an exceptional teacher.

The wise act without effort and teach by example.

Tao Te Ching

Trashing Lilly

Lilly's Social Science class was still in progress, when I reached the building.

What I heard coming out of that room on that day, and two days before, was student discussion, something pretty rare in an education environment where we are taught to sit in our row and only ask the most necessary questions for fear of getting on the wrong side of the teacher by irritating him or her in their planned presentation. Lilly's students talked freely, as if they were with a big sister. Her classes were predominantly young women, mostly Hispanic, given the community in which the school was located. Sometimes Lilly spoke Spanish for clarity.

The chairs were in a circle and Lilly was one of the circle. The discussion was lively and Lilly had illustrated her points with notes on the board. After it was over, I complimented her on the way the students participated and asked if she would mind if I sat in sometimes when I got there early.

It was an illuminating experience to watch her relate the book they were reading, not a standard textbook, to key points she had previously written on the board, and there was a sense of trust you could feel. Unlike so many classes, her students seemed completely relaxed in the presence of each other and their teacher.

We got to know each other a little over two or three semesters. She was a mother with one child and another on the way and she would have to leave a month before school was over because she needed rest in preparation for delivery.

She was the best of what a teacher should be. She trusted and respected her students and shared the authority of the classroom freely with them. She had no buttons that could be pushed and she was completely open to what her students had to say, never worrying about whether she was the authority maintaining control. I didn't see her again until the next semester in the fall when, again, we used the same room. She had had a healthy little boy. It was then she spoke about what had happened when she left for maternity leave.

"I prepared a series of lessons and put them in a binder with notes for each class period. I wanted the students to have continuity. The day before I left I gave them to the full-time male instructor who would be finishing the semester for me. A week later I started getting distressing emails from the girls in the class.

"It seemed that on the first day the new instructor came ten minutes late. He was carrying the notebook I had prepared. He put down his brief case and addressed the students. Looking at the notebook he said, 'Your former teacher gave me this to get us through the rest of the semester.' He looked at each student and then walked over to the trash can by the door into which he dropped my notes and, from what they said, he smiled."

Within a few months, Lilly found a full-time teaching job that she loves. She will always serve as an example of what a great teacher is.

The Silencers

I was again cursed with that rectangular classroom where the heating system was either too hot or too cold. Nothing but blank walls and rows of tables where the students were forced to sit, perhaps preparing them for their time in the work place: show up on time, do your work, live for "hump day," (Wednesday), live for weekends.

The class was almost sixty and was at first probably the most challenging I had ever had when it comes to discipline. Normally I had never had such problems because I give an equal amount of authority in conducting the class to the students. But this class, from day one, was different. I had drawn six members of the school football team and they were all Afro-American, with a streak of cockiness. I tried to call roll and they would be jiving with each other. But then the talking spread. Actually, the solution was fairly easy. I asked them to stay after class in the second week because I wanted to ask them a favor.

They reluctantly came to the front tables and lounged about, waiting, almost daring me.

"Here's the deal. I can't teach if there is a lot of noise in the classroom. You guys know that. So," I paused, "I want to give you guys an assignment if you will take it." This piqued their interest and slowly they all came to an erect posture.

"Like what is it, man?"

"What I need is for you to be a designated group of silencers. Whenever there is talk anywhere in class, I want one of you to quietly go to where it is and tell the people to be quiet. We're in college now not high school. I'll let the whole class know this next time that I have given you this authority. What do you say?"

They looked at each other and a series of smiles came to their faces. "You mean we can tell other students to knock off the chatter?"

"Right, and you will naturally be the ones who set the example."

They looked at each other. "We can dig it."

"Good. Thanks."

Within a week, the six had quietly let it be known that they were serious and weren't going to be messed with. It went from the noisiest class I have taught to the quietest. It's about respect, but more than that it's unfortunately about time and money. In the next vignette, the reality of time and money almost made Jed Gonzales forget his education.

Your Money or Your Education

When you teach at the junior college level, especially in a community where many people suffer the poverty salaries of service and farm labor jobs, money many times hinders bright minds because they are at the mercy of a low wage employer who, naturally, cares first about his or her business and second about a young employee's attempt to go to school at the same time. Education for many offers a way of life none of their ancestors have had. So, to many, the phrase can be phrased as "Your Money or Your Education." Jed was one of those students.

He was engaged from the first day, participating in class discussions, offering fine insights. His first paper was astounding to say the least. But for his lack of funds and parental motivation (neither parent had a high school degree), he, like Audi, had managed to gain the very most from a public high school education. His writing was very clear. His analysis would have ranked with that of a student at one of the country's elite colleges. I told him that on his first paper, giving him not a 100, but a 110 for exceptional work. He came up after the fourth class when I returned the first papers.

"I don't quite understand the grade. I never got a 110 before."

"Well, Jed, 100 is perfect and 110 is more than perfect. Comprende?"

He nodded. "It's just that I have this thing with my work. I live at home but have to pay for school and help my family as well. My Dad's a gardener, and he fell out of a tree a few months ago and probably won't be able to work for at least six months more according to the doctor. He was self-employed so there was little Workers' Comp or any other aid from the state or federal government. I'm trying to help pick up the slack and go to school too. This is my last semester before I transfer to the university. I have to work a lot of hours."

"I recommend to all my students that if they have to work more than go to school less or vice-versa." I knew that was easy to say but I also knew that Jed had no choice. "Do you have any idea what you want to do?"

"Something in medicine, if I qualify."

"I'll try to help you out as best I can but I also need to be fair to the other students. I'm sure you understand."

"Yeah, I do."

"Let me know if I can do anything." He nodded and left.

From that point onward the quality of his work slowly deteriorated. I wrote detailed notes why his assignments were lacking but the quality just kept dropping. He managed to get a C in the class when he was more than an A student.

When I said good-bye at the end of the semester, he told me he had been working sixty-five hours a week at two jobs. He was managing the swing shift at a local McDonald's and trying to take care of his father's gardening clients during the day. I wished him well.

As sometimes happens, I receive emails from students after a class has ended. About four months later, I got one from him. He had gotten a hardship scholarship from the university and now only had to work twenty-five hours a week to support himself. His father and Jed's younger brother were back doing his father's gardening business. He said it took a while to actually sleep all night, but his grades had improved and he knew he could maintain them and his scholarship.

Jed Gonzales had gotten the money to get his life back.

In order to rationalize our industrial-military complex, we have to destroy our capacity to see clearly anymore what is in front of, and to imagine what is beyond, our noses.

R. D. Laing

Breathing, Eating a Cookie and Finding Rain in a Sheet of Paper

By modern or ancient standards, the semester long assignment was strange for a U.S. History class. Every two weeks on Monday a single page essay was due on Thich Nhat Hanh's book *Peace Is Every Step*. The actual assignment was to read one of the short essays by this Vietnamese Buddhist monk, give your impression of it and do so in a setting in nature like a park or beach, without the possession of any electronic gadgets like a cell phone. The purpose was to separate the students from the holographic world of plastic they all were daily living in and get them back into the reality of nature. To say the least, it's always a struggle.

The second half of the quiz was to record the student's spontaneous impressions of the natural setting in which they chose to be. The first essay was assigned and the rest were the choice of the student.

The assigned essay was called "Interbeing" and told the story of how the piece of paper it was written on was first a cloud, then rain, then a tree, then a sawmill and so on. The result was hopeful, but the hope took a while to materialize: not because of lack of intelligence, but because of lack of exposure to the natural world.

The "Interbeing" essay was a revelation to most students because it showed how no paper could exist without everything from the rain cloud to the delivery truck taking the paper to distribution points. It included all the interactions of people along the way and the monk summed up the effort as "Interbeing." The students who really understood the assignment wrote about those interrelations. The students who didn't grasp it at first just made a rote list of each component of the process.

One comment that stood out was, "These relationships not only exist between each other, but also relate further to my presence in nature; each part of the natural world, from me, to the stone, to tree, to bird somehow play a part in making this forest what it is. If you take one away, the picture becomes distorted."

A common comment that emerged by the sixth week and third essay illustrated that these students had really not lost touch, except on a temporary basis. The first essays complained of "going naked" without their electronic plastic, but by number three the majority exclaimed that they were "actually relieved that I didn't bring my cell phone along. I never realized how tied to it I was but without it there was only the quiet of the beach and the waves and the soft wind around me. That made me feel lighter."

The essay that the majority wrote on at different times was one titled "Cookie of Childhood." It was about the monk when he was a small boy and his mother would bring him a cookie from the market which he would take out to the grass and lie in the sun with his dog and cat against his legs.

He would take over half an hour to eat it. The majority realization was "I never realized how fast I eat. I tried eating a cookie and it was gone in three seconds." But the majority realization also was "I made myself take ten minutes to eat a cookie. It was weird. I took it outside with my new puppy who kept trying to take it from me until finally I got him to stop and I could eat it in the sun. As I ate slowly, I realized that I seldom tasted my food. But now I did. And even more, I was aware of my surroundings: the lawn, my favorite oak tree I was leaning against, with my dog by my side and the feel of the grass against my legs as I sat in the warm sun."

There were many who said they wished they could do without their plastic gadgets and just eat a cookie and feel the natural world around them and stop living such a stressful life. That seems easier the younger you are, even for a six year old.

A Six Year Old's Wisdom

In order to balance the onslaught of plastic in student's lives--the isolation they are creating for themselves by avoiding face to face experience--I create an exercise that brings them back into reality as best I can. The exercise, which I discussed in the previous vignette is to leave all electronic equipment behind and go out into nature, whether that be a park, beach, the sea or mountains, and just sit in the silence and read a single essay from Thich Nhat Hanh's book *Peace Is Every Step* and write a one page essay that discusses what the essay meant to the student and what his or her thoughts were while sitting in nature.

It takes a while for them to figure out that there is no right answer, but eventually, and with my constant repetition, they realize that there is no right answer. That's when they relax and I begin receiving some amazing and deeply introspective work.

Anna Flores was from a large, poor and struggling family. She worked thirty hours a week, helped babysit her younger siblings, cared for her aging grandmother and attended school, carrying twelve units. One of her essays centered round the abuse we put upon the earth.

"I decided to write this essay at the park near my house. It is usually empty during the week and since the weather was warm, I decided to sit under a big tree in the shade where the grass must have been cut the previous day. As I read my assignment, I was stopped by an unusually loud amount of noise. Most of the time it is very quiet there and easy to concentrate.

There was a birthday party that was just breaking up and the children and adults were passing the trash cans before going to their cars.

What amazed me was how much of the trash never made it into the cans, and very few tried to put the items that could be recycled into that bin, even though it was there in plain sight.

When they drove off, I thought about my essay on respecting the earth and I decided to go over to the bins and pick up the trash on the ground and put it in its proper place. The first thing I noticed was a lot of wasted food. It didn't take me long to do the job. I washed my hands in the restroom close by and realized I had to get home. There was no more time to meditate on what I had read.

I went straight to my six year old sister's school not far from the house and we walked home together. On the way I noticed a plastic container and unconsciously picked it up. My little sister asked why I was doing that and I told her we would put the plastic in our recycle can at home. She asked to carry it and when we got home she put it in the bin.

I am really the only one who recycles at home and started just after beginning these nature writings.

After dinner, I was helping my mother with the dishes before studying and my little sister was watching us. My Mother was just about to throw a plastic dish into the trash. My little sister jumped off the stool where she was sitting and said, 'Give me that, I will put it in our recycle bin. You should know better Mommy."

> *The highest truth cannot be put into words. Therefore, the greatest teacher has nothing to say. He/She simply gives of themselves in service and never worries.*
>
> Lao Tzu

The Crippled Boy

It was a large class, perhaps fifty or more, and he sat in the front row in his motorized chair. He could only operate it with his right hand because he had partial use of his body, just enough to move his legs and shift himself in the deep black leather chair.

He was twenty-two and had been injured in a car accident when another car broadsided the one he was riding in, and it did permanent damage to his spine and body in general so that his speech sounded like he was gasping for breath. It was more like a whine and you had to listen very carefully in order to hear the flow and meaning of his words. It was very painful to see him struggle to make a point.

I am unable to reproduce that speech except to say it initially, and each time, sent a wave of discomfort through me, and I hoped at the same time that he would say what his point was and get through it with as little pain or embarrassment as possible.

Before the accident, he had been described as "brilliant" by teachers that knew him; brilliant, articulate, fully engaged in the lecture, challenging, and contributing often. In other words, the ideal student. But now he could just sit there bent over slightly and sometimes raise his head to make a point. And those points were insightful, even in his condition, but hard for the class to understand, so I tried often to repeat what he had said while pretending to rephrase it.

What was gratifying was the way many of my students tried to listen. Some would bend forward, some would offer comments, which always brought the best kind of a smile that he could make to his face.

I had many talks with the counseling department and after two semesters changes had to be made. He was just unable to work in the classroom environment. The decision was to try to find a learning situation that would be best for him.

Here was a brilliant mind that would never realize itself and there was nothing I could do to help. I would see him around the campus, usually alone tooling along the pathways. Once he motioned to me and I went over to say hello. He awkwardly extended his hand and I shook it. He looked up at me with his crooked look and smiled.

"Yah….yah," he stammered, "Yah…weeeerre best tea…teacher"

I had always felt that I failed him.

SETTING THEM FREE: NOTES ON TEACHING   71

In the late Jonathan Winter's first record album, he did a skit in which a landing craft full of Marines is approaching possibly the Normandy Beaches of World War II. He does several impersonations of the men and they are very funny until the front of the craft opens and the Marines charge into the sound of mortar and gunfire. The last voice you hear is an Afro-American Marine who exclaims with utter surprise, "These people is tryin' to kill us!"

Sitting With a World War II Veteran

I had just lectured on WWI and II and left the class with a question, "Next time we will talk about whether it was worth it or not, so give it some thought and we'll see what we come up with." I was gathering up my notes when I noticed that one of the students still remained sitting in the front row. "Can I help you with something?"

"Actually I was going to tell you about one of the patients at the elder care center where I work. He is one of the last veterans from World War II." I pulled up a seat. She was a beautiful Hispanic girl with kind and open eyes and there was a natural and deep sense of compassion in her smile.

"A lot of the people who work there don't like talking to him. He has some dementia but it really doesn't seem too bad. He just likes to talk about his time in the war but I don't mind. It's not that he's nutty or anything."

"What does he talk about with you?"

"That's what you're asking, 'was it worth it,' reminded me of. He mostly talks about how much he regrets what he did and what he experienced. He's never proud of himself like so many veterans we've had there. They're always bragging about being the greatest generation because they fought in the Second World War. He just says over and over that if he had to do it over he would have gone to prison instead of joining up."

"What do you make of that?" She shrugged. "I don't know. He has no family who come and see him. He just needs someone to talk to now and then. I don't mind."

"You think he would have gone to prison?"

She paused and stared at the blackboard. Almost a minute passed. "Yeah, yes, I think he would have because I've heard him argue about the Iraq War with other Vets who defend the government's action there. He really gets excited about that. Yes, I believe he would have gone to jail."

"He must not be very popular with the other Vets."

She shook her head. "They stay clear of him. Is that what you mean by 'was it worth it?' Like sacrificing your life to go to jail instead of going to fight?"

"That's got to be part of it I would think."

"I guess." She got up, picking up her backpack. "Thanks"

"No, thank you."

I Think I'm a Liberal; Should I Buy a Gun?

That was the question that Alberto asked me one day after the rest of the class had left. He had joined the Army for eight years. In return, he would receive a grant that might pay his way through the last two years of college. He was always seeing the connections in history and it surprised him how little the United States had learned from our part in history: how we kept repeating the same mistakes over and over.

"No, I think you should find another Castro somewhere and go into the mountains with him to fight against some political puppet the U.S. had placed in his country." I smiled and he got the joke, smiling back. "Why do you think you need a gun? I didn't think liberals carried guns."

"I'm talking about self-defense."

"They'll give you a gun and more when you finally join up," I added.

"But that's a different kind of self-defense."

"What's the difference?" I drew two stick figures on the board, each pointing a gun at the other.

"Well, one's the enemy and the other is a countryman of mine who just has different political views."

"Then what does your enemy have that you feel like killing him for?"

Alberto sat there with his head bent down for a couple of minutes as if the table top would reveal an answer. "His ideals, I would say."

"But doesn't your countryman, the conservative guy, have ideals you don't like too?"

He laughed. "So you're telling me I need guns for both of them?"

"What about no gun for either since you'd really be killing them pretty much for the same reason wouldn't you; you disagreed with both of them."

"Well, but the enemy wants to take over my country."

"Do you really believe that a guy much like yourself would want to kill you if he knew you? Do you think you're that unlikeable?"

He shook his head. "You're getting me confused. We started all this because I thought I needed a gun because I am liberal."

"Right. But what's liberal?"

He looked at me with a little suspicion. "Someone who is pro-choice and for reducing the influence of business on government and the rich. Stuff like that."

"Okay, but isn't the definition of both pretty close? Conservatives want to preserve and make safe. I think that's what liberals want too?"

"Yeah. They just want it in different ways but how do we bring them together."

"How about we listen openly, not defensively to each other for starters?"

"So you're telling me I really don't need a gun?"

"I'm also telling you to find a Castro and go into the hills and fight with him for the right of the poor and common people and de-enlist from the army." I smiled.

"You're kidding, right?"

"Well, eight years in the military is no joke."

He waved and left. I don't know if we solved his problem. I will be waiting for an email. I hope it comes from the mountains of Central America where he is fighting and trying to overthrow an unjust dictator supported by powerful interests.

I Was Wondering About My Grade

Toward the end of one semester, I received this from a top student who had completed all her work except a few minor quizzes which wouldn't affect her grade. She had one more paper to write.

This is Jane Larson from your survey class. I'm writing for a couple reasons. One, I was wondering what my grade was for The Things They Carried paper. Two, I wanted to explain why I missed two days the other week and couldn't pick up my paper. As you know my husband had an appointment with the doctor which I attended. That was Monday. On Wednesday, he was horribly sick from said appointment as it was a biopsy of a mass in his neck. Now since then, we've learned that he has thyroid cancer. This, as you can imagine, has been a little hard on us. I honestly don't have time to do the quizzes that are left that you've assigned. I can most likely complete the paper due at the end of the semester, and will attend the final session. I honestly need to know if these lack of quizzes will affect my grade detrimentally. I really want an A and need to know what is the minimum I'd have to do to achieve that? Thank you for understanding.

Thanks,

Jane Larson

Dear Jane,

There are four more sessions of the class remaining, but you are finished now. You have no more work to do except love and support your husband. You have an A in the class and need not attend anymore, including *the final session, nor write the last paper. Medicine continues to improve, including the healing of cancer. An older woman I know had the same thing years ago at 21 and she has so far lived another 40 years. My heart goes out to you both. Try as best you can to keep the faith, whatever that may be for you. Please, keep in touch.*

All good,
Roger

What Are Grades Anyway?

It was the last day of class. Not a real class but what is always called "finals." I have found that finals are nothing more than a teacher justifying his or her salary. Not so much in math, science and language where the subjects really dictate memorization, but some of the social sciences like history where finals go in one ear and out the other.

Kara had missed turning in some quizzes during the year and did not turn in one of the longer papers which were worth 50% of the grade. Yet she had been there every class session and I knew she was listening, recording some of it that might pop into her head years later unannounced. I had written among other things on the last paper which she turned in, "Eighty-seven. Nice job analyzing the chapters in question. Course grade D."

She waited until all the other students had said good-bye and gotten their questions answered. Then she approached timidly.

The soft glisten of tears were in her eyes. "I know I missed the quizzes and the papers. I was stupid. But isn't there anything I can do to make up for that a little?"

"You know it wouldn't be fair to others if I let people do that."

"I know. I know." By now the tears were truly visible. "I was just hoping. I know I had to work too many hours. That was stupid too. I know you said 'take less classes and work more or visa-versa'. But I had no choice. My Dad's hours were cut way back. I told you that."

"I know but you knew the policy."

She looked down at her paper and up at me. A tear or two came down her cheeks. She shook her head, "I know." She started to turn away.

"I'm sorry, Kara." She tried to smile, then quickly left the room.

Two days later I began to enter the grades for all my classes into the computer. She was in the second class of about thirty-five. I entered a D in the box and moved on until I finished all the grades for that class. I was about to put my grade reports into my school file. I stopped.

She was a young girl like so many of my students, from poor families, maybe the first to enter college, struggling.

I went to the bathroom to wash my hands. I looked into the mirror a long time. Finally I shook by head and reopened the file with Kara's grade in it. I changed it to a C.

Afterward

I would like to conclude this work by rededicating myself to my students who have been the inspiration for this work and for my teaching. They continue to astonish me with their amazing insights, which are so often lost under the regime of authority. My students' comments and evaluations have been so much of the motivation to keep teaching well and honest, and I have included some of these, not for self-praise but for the love they have returned to me. What they have said means more to me than the evaluations of any administrators.

Finally, I would like to take a moment to thank those teachers who are really on the front line of education facing so often impossible tasks without financial support. Those are the teachers from kindergarten through ninth grade who are the real heroes of education, the least recognized, the first to blame and the poorest paid.

The reason I teach is to help students in my small and sometimes unpredictable way to unveil their true spirits and have the courage to realize their own truths, as some of these vignettes show, and allow these truths to unfold in living their lives.

As long as society is willing to view education from a business agenda, the longer the ongoing negative experiences of our world will increase and persist. If education isn't put first, we will continue slowly killing ourselves and our planet.

From the Love of My Students

This letter is in regards to Mr. Simpson. Although I believe he deserves much more than kind words, that's all I have to offer at this time. Roger as a person and as a teacher has had an enormous part of making me who I am today.

What Roger teaches is far beyond what any book, information site, or even what our parents can teach us. The way he incorporates American culture, history, the state of the earth and how we are all an integral part of making the earth what it is or can be is simply beautiful. He is very unique and empowers us to be responsible and powerful human beings.

I guess what I am trying to say is that we are incredibly fortunate to have him at this college, not only as a teacher, a colleague or a mentor; but also as a friend.

Respectfully Yours,
Amanda Rae C.

Roger,

I just wanted to let you know how much I appreciate you and your teaching skills. You have been my best teacher here, and when I think of the great ones throughout the years you will definitely make the list. You have been understanding, thoughtful and encouraging. I thank you for all of these things. You have made me want to continue to pursue my education. I always knew I wanted to continue but wasn't sure it was attainable. But you made me think twice about it and I know this will only be a start. And the feedback you have given me from my writings has always been encouraging. I feel like you understand my life when I put it on paper.

Take care of yourself and I hope to see you again soon!
Alexandra M.

These are just a few examples of the kind of love that keeps me teaching.

Teaching as if Learning Mattered

Had education ever worked, there would be no poverty

People would rise and feed the children they love

The air would be polished blue

the sun yellow

the moon marble

the ocean as clear as lakes

the lakes as clear as the Indians once saw

Had education ever worked

Anxiety would only be in the uncertainty of a farmer's weather

"Crime," a word unknown in the language

Nor "violence"

Had education ever…

Corporations would be communities

Where humans were respected, not abused

Communities would be human and whole,

Competition would be only within:

a slow walk by the river,

rubbing oil into the chair you just built,

an hour's fishing and meditating,

Salmon upstream and bears in shallow water

The list is almost infinite

But "ever" isn't "never"

Education and Learning can begin to be

www.ingramcontent.com/pod-product-compliance
Lightning Source LLC
Chambersburg PA
CBHW061501040426
42450CB00008B/1446